2 BOOSTING ENERGY

8 POWER WEEK

10 SPRINGTIME

22 COOL SUMMER COCKTAILS

30 HEALTH DRINKS

38 VITALITY SHAKES

50 WINTER WARMERS

GAIA

Boosting

with home-made drinks

Energy

100 Per cent Enjoyment

Drink yourself fit, become more active, and feel healthier with energy drinks that you can make yourself from fruit juices, fresh dairy produce, and aromatic herbal teas. Pure juice lets you enjoy the full flavour. Don't settle for sweetened, diluted juices that are sold as nectars, fruit juice drinks, or cordials. Check the label. It should always read "100 per cent juice", so you can dilute it to taste. Freshly squeezed juices also contain nothing but pure juice and have one big advantage: unlike many fruit juices, they are not based on fruit juice concentrates, which are evaporated and rediluted and thus lose much of their flavour and essential nutrients.

More Water than Juice

Although a nectar may sound natural and pure, such drinks usually consist of more than 50 per cent water, and contain only half as many essential nutrients as pure juice. Fruit juice drinks may contain only 5 per cent juice. A lot of sugar, sweeteners, flavours and acids are used to make up for the lack of fruit flavour. Thus an artificial sweet thirst-quencher, has very little nutritional value and sometimes contains more calories than pure juice. And, as with fruit juices, vegetable juices can be pure, or diluted and with other additives, so it's important to read the label.

Finding Juices

Try health food or wholefood stores and well-stocked off-licences in your search for 100 per cent taste. You may find pure strawberry, apricot, raspberry, cherry, and even elderflower juice on the shelves. However, you will search in vain for some pure fruit and most pure vegetable juices. So why not make the juice yourself?

Smoothies

Smoothies are fruit juices blended usually with some yoghurt or skimmed milk. They may contain some sugar and water, but on the whole, smoothies are an easy and appetising way to get valuable nutrients into the diet, and count towards the 5-a-day fruit and vegetable recommendation now put forward by health experts.

Yoghurt is a particularly healthy ingredient as it contains lactic acid bacteria that convert natural sugars into lactic acid. Lactic acid can combat the growth of harmful bacteria and strengthen the body's defences. Particular health-giving strains of bacteria are now also available in special fermented milk drinks available in the chiller cabinet. These may help prevent infections and gastric problems, and may even help lower a high cholesterol level.

Squeezing or Pureeing

Raw fruit and vegetables contain more essential nutrients than their juices, because commercial juices are generally pasteurized to improve their shelf life. Fresh orange or grapefruit juice, which is richer in nutrients, can be made very easily using just a lemon squeezer and a twist of the wrist. Berry fruits, kiwi fruit, bananas, mangoes, melons, and many varieties of vegetable can be puréed using just a basic hand-held blender and a little liquid. Then either press the purée through a sieve, or dilute it with another juice, and you will have all the essential nutrients in a glass. If you develop a taste for fresh fruit juices, then invest in a juicing machine, which produces fresh juice from fruit and vegetables in seconds. This book contains simple recipes for which you need only a hand-held blender.

RECOMMENDATION: Use organic produce wherever possible. If you wish to avoid genetically modified (GM) foods, read any labels with care and select certified organic produce, as this is not produced from GM ingredients.

Natural Active

for a healthy mind and body

Ingredients

FRUIT JUICE STRENGTHENS DEFENCES

Juices strengthen the body, primarily as a result of their vitamin C and beta-carotene content. Both essential nutrients prevent the formation of free radicals, which develop due to the action of pollutants, stress, and UV radiation, and then attack the body's cells. Carotinoids and flavonoids, two important groups among a wealth of highly effective plant substances, are also contained in juices. They heal primary damage caused by free radicals, preventing the cells under attack from metamorphosing into cancerous cells. Carotinoids are found particularly in orange-fleshed fruit such as peaches, mangoes and canteloupe melon. Flavonoids are concentrated in the pith of citrus fruits, just under the skin, so don't discard this part.

KEEP ACTIVE

Many people who play sport in their spare time, and those trying to get fitter, have experienced painful muscle cramps. Muscles complain when they need more minerals to be able to continue working at maximum efficiency. Massage and heat are the best ways to disperse cramp quickly. When doing any kind of exercise, the body also loses minerals as it sweats, in particular magnesium and potassium. The most enjoyable way for sporty types to replace these minerals is with fresh fruit and vegetable cocktails. Thanks to a combination of vegetables, herbs, and the right fruits, these are packed full of minerals. The drinks also replace the liquid which the body loses in the form of sweat when playing tennis, playing football, jogging, cycling, or when in the gym. Pure juice is too concentrated and does not contain enough water to replace the liquid lost as sweat. Sportsmen and women should dilute pure juices with water, preferably with mineral water with a high magnesium content. Energy drinks need not contain much protein. Those who play sports for a hobby can replace the protein lost during exercise with a normal meal.

DRINK AWAY YOUR STRESS

Stress may affect people in two ways: when life is a mad whirl and people are under pressure, there are those who console themselves with chocolate and crisps, and those who forget to eat at all. Both reactions are unhealthy. Steady your nerves with plenty of food that builds you up, such as milk shakes. Even if your nerves are stretched to breaking point, the vitamin B2 in dairy produce will never let you down. Buttermilk aids concentration by supplying an extra dose of lecithin. If you want to counteract stress with a pick-me-up, you need long-lasting carbohydrates (from bananas, for example), or lots of vitamin C from oranges, kiwi fruit, or broccoli.

Healthy Digestion

If your bowels and stomach are playing you up, it's a sign of neglect. A few juice drinks can correct minor ailments thanks to the roughage and lactic acid they contain, or because they provide lots of fluid. What they can't do, however, is combat the real reasons for your problems. If you are plagued by stomach aches, then you should forego cold cocktails.

Detoxification

The more fluid the kidneys have to remove, the more metabolic waste product can be excreted by the body, and water with it. This process is known as detoxification and takes the pressure off the heart and circulation. Inner cleansing need be neither nasty nor monotonous. Cleansing drinks contain potassium—rich fruits or vegetables and, above all, lots of water. The more water you drink, the better.

Drink

Drinks for every occasion

Aid

Who wouldn't like simply to drink away their ailments? With the right drink, you might just do that! The detailed tables will help you to choose the right cocktail. Most of them will help your immune system or keep you mentally fit. Other drinks contain lots of minerals, but not too much sugar, which is just right for keen sports players. If you have gastric problems, you will find drinks that keep the stomach and bowels healthy with yoghurt or roughage. And if you want to "detox", it's a good idea to drink juices that contain lots of potassium, or a combination of herbal tea and fruit juice. The choice is yours. Why not try a variety of drinks to find your favourite? You'll soon be won over.

NOTE: If you are ill you need to consult a doctor. Energy drinks are no substitute for medical advice or prescribed medicines.
TIP: Use a plastic or stainless steel sieve when sieving acidic fruit or vegetable purées.

DETOXIFYING DRINKS

Anti-Influenza Punch
Apple-Linden Blossom Punch
Apricot & Apple Whey Drink
Berry Bowl with Fruit Juice
Broccoli, Pear & Pineapple Juice Drink
Camomile-Citrus Punch
Cucumber-Melon Milk
Dill-Vegetable Drink
Exotic Energy Cocktail
Fennel-Exotic Fruit Punch
Fruit Fantasy Cocktail
Fruity Strawberry Shake
Green Card Cocktail
Lamb's Lettuce Buttermilk Shake
Pink Kiwi Colada
Radish-Kohlrabi Cocktail
Spicy Vegetable Drink
Sweet Buttermilk Shake
Winter Delight Punch

DRINKS FOR ACTIVE PEOPLE AND SPORTS ENTHUSIASTS

Berry Bowl with Fruit Juice
Cucumber-Melon Milk
Dill-Vegetable Drink
Green Card Cocktail
Lamb's Lettuce Buttermilk Shake
Mango Yoghurt Ice in Pineapple Koumiss
Pink Kiwi Colada
Radish-Kohlrabi Cocktail
Sea Buckthorn-Sage Punch

STRESSBUSTERS

Apricot & Apple Whey Drink

Banana Fig Milk

Berry-Banana Shake

Buttermilk-Coconut Shake

Cucumber-Melon Milk

Drive-in Drink

Exotic Energy Cocktail

Fruity Strawberry Shake

Good Mood Mixture

Green Card Cocktail

Highway to Holiday

Lamb's Lettuce Buttermilk Shake

Night Owl Cocktail

Pineapple Almond Milk

Plum Yoghurt Shake

Radish-Kohlrabi Cocktail

Raspberry-Buttermilk Shake

Red Panther's Punch

Rose-Red Koumiss Drink

Sea Buckthorn-Sage Punch

Spicy Vegetable Drink

Sun-Blocker Cocktail

Sweet Buttermilk Shake

Vitality Fruit Cocktail

White Wellness Shake

White, Red & Green Drink

IMMUNITY-BOOSTING DRINKS

Anti-Influenza Punch

Apple-Linden Blossom Punch

Blue Hour Orchard Cocktail

Camomile-Citrus Punch

Caribbean Coconut Cocktail

Dill-Vegetable Drink

Drive-in Drink

Exotic Energy Cocktail

Fennel-Exotic Fruit Punch

Fresh Spring Breeze

Good Morning Alarm Call

Kiwi Fruit Shake with Melon Ice

Night Owl Cocktail

Pink Kiwi Colada

Quick & Easy Drink

Red Panther's Punch

Red Pepper Power

Sea Buckthorn-Sage Punch

Slight Summer Dream

Spicy Vegetable Drink

Strawberry-Mango Cooler

Sun-Blocker Cocktail

Sweet Iron-Man

White Wellness Shake

Winter Delight Punch

DRINKS FOR THE DIGESTION

Anti-Influenza Punch

Apple-Linden Blossom Punch

Apricot-Apple Whey Drink

Banana Fig Milk

Broccoli, Pear & Pineapple Juice

Drive-in Drink

Fresh Spring Breeze

Fruit Fantasy Cocktail

Orchard Cocktail

Fruity Strawberry Shake

Green Card Cocktail

Kiwi Fruit Shake with Melon Ice

Mango Yoghurt Ice in Pineapple Koumiss

Plum Yoghurt Shake

Raspberry Buttermilk Shake

Rose-Red Koumiss Drink

Sea Buckthorn-Sage Punch

Spicy Vegetable Drink

Sweet Iron-Man

Vitality Fruit Cocktail

Winter Delight Punch

Yoghurt Pick-me-up

Power

for improved health and wellbeing

Week

DRINK YOURSELF FIT!

Do you suffer from tiredness, poor concentration, and bad moods? Then what you need is a Power Week with lots of fresh cocktails. No matter how great the stress you are under, three energy drinks a day, quick to squeeze and mixed in moments, will lend you new energy. Three small boosts in the form of classic, simple mixtures of juices, milk, or herbal teas will increase your activity level and help prevent afternoon lows, seasonal affective disorders, and other kinds of common depressions.

EAT AND DRINK SPARINGLY

Unfortunately, even the best drinks will be to no avail if you eat the wrong kind of diet. A diet rich in fat and protein damages the body, wastes energy, and provides far too many calories. You should therefore eat less fatty meat, and more lean meat and fish; less processed meat and more low-fat cottage cheese. And try very low-fat spreads, pickles, or low-fat dressings on your bread, rather than butter or dairy spreads, or do without altogether. You can never have enough vegetables, fruit, pasta, potatoes, rice, and wholemeal bread in a healthy diet. They provide masses of carbohydrates, so that muscles and brain cells have a supply of readily available fuel and stay active.

NOTHING CAN GO WRONG

Juices also contain many carbohydrates and so are ideally suited to a health-conscious diet. Three types of juice a day are specified in the weekly diet. The three juices go well together, but if you don't like one of them, don't have the ingredients to hand, or you don't have time to make them, then two different types of juice are perfectly acceptable. Simply prepare double the quantity of one of them, which you should then drink twice a day. The juices for the morning (first suggestion) and evening (last suggestion) each take a little more time to prepare, while the suggested lunchtime juice can be mixed in no time at all. The list also contains the right drinks to meet the needs of children, party-goers, and other groups with special requirements, which can be effortlessly incorporated into the week's plan.

WEEKLY PLAN

Monday

❋ White Wellness Shake ❋ Buttermilk Coconut Shake❋ Fennel-Exotic Fruit Punch

Tuesday

❋ Good Morning Alarm Call ❋ Sweet Iron-Man ❋ Red Pepper Power

Wednesday

❋ Rose-Red Koumiss Drink ❋ Fruit Fantasy Cocktail ❋Camomile-Citrus Punch

Thursday

❋ Quick & Easy Drink ❋ Sweet Buttermilk Shake ❋ Spicy Vegetable Drink

Friday

❋ Pink Kiwi Colada ❋ Drive-in Drink ❋ White, Red & Green Drink

Saturday

❋ Sun-Blocker Cocktail ❋ Banana Fig Milk ❋ Night Owl Cocktail

Sunday

❋ Red Panther's Punch ❋ Berry Bowl with Fruit Juice ❋ Apple-Linden Blossom Punch

For morning grouches

Drive-in Drink ❋ Fresh Spring Breeze ❋ Good Mood Mixture ❋ Good Morning
Alarm Call ❋ Quick & Easy Drink ❋ Vitality Fruit Cocktail

For tireless night owls

Berry-Banana Drink ❋ Dill-Vegetable Drink ❋ Green Card Cocktail ❋ Night Owl
Cocktail ❋ Spicy Vegetable Drink ❋ Red Pepper Power

For fit kids

Exotic Energy Cocktail ❋ Fruity Strawberry Shake ❋ Good Mood Mixture ❋
Highway to Holiday ❋ Raspberry Buttermilk Shake ❋ Red Panther's Punch

For increased concentration

Pineapple-Almond Milk ❋ Banana Fig Milk ❋ Berry-Banana Shake ❋ Sweet Iron-
Man ❋ White Wellness Drink ❋ Winter Delight Punch

Exotic Energy Cocktail

made with four varieties

of fresh fruit

Ingredients for 2 Drinks: • 1 small papaya • 4 kiwi fruit • 2 oranges • 1 grapefruit • 1 vanilla pod • lightly chilled mineral water

Peel the papaya, then cut it in half and scoop out the seeds. Peel the kiwi fruit, reserving two large slices for decoration. Purée the papaya and kiwi fruit until very smooth. Remove the peel from the oranges in a very thin spiral with a zester or canelle knife. Squeeze the juice from the grapefruit and oranges. Combine the fruit juices and purée. Slit the vanilla pod in half lengthwise and scrape out the seeds. Add them to the fruit mixture. Dilute the fruit mixture to taste with mineral water, and divide it equally between two tall glasses. Make a cut from the middle of each slice of kiwi fruit to the edge, and perch one slice on the rim of each glass. Decorate the rim of each glass with orange peel spirals. Serve with straws.

EQUIPMENT: HAND-HELD BLENDER • LEMON SQUEEZER • 2 TALL GLASSES • 2 STRAWS

power

White

with natural minerals for fitness

Wellness Shake

Ingredients for 2 drinks: • 2 kiwi fruit • 1 banana • 100ml (3 1/2 fl oz) buttermilk •

150ml (5fl oz) apple juice • mineral water • vanilla sugar • grated chocolate

Peel the kiwi fruit and banana and slice them, reserving a few slices of each for

decoration. Purée the remaining sliced fruit with the buttermilk and apple juice. Stir

in mineral water if liked. Add vanilla sugar to taste. Pour into glasses, then decorate

with slices of kiwi fruit and banana, and sprinkle grated chocolate on top.

EQUIPMENT: HAND-HELD BLENDER

power

Red Panther's

a wild mixture of papaya purée and carrot juice

Punch

Ingredients for 2 drinks: • 1/2 Papaya • 100ml (3 1/2 fl oz) pear juice • 100ml (3 1/2 fl oz) orange

juice • 100ml (3 1/2 fl oz) carrot juice

Peel the papaya and scoop out the seeds. Cut off two thin segments for decoration.

Chop the remaining flesh small and purée it with the three juices. Pour the juice into

glasses. Make a cut in each of the papaya segments, and perch one on the rim of

each glass. Serve with a straw.

EQUIPMENT: HAND-HELD BLENDER • WIDE STRAWS

power

Good Morning

vital nutrients for a bright start

Alarm Call

Wash the orange and pat it dry. Using a very sharp knife or canelle knife, cut the peel away from the orange in a very thin spiral and reserve it. Slice the orange in half and juice it.

Slice the melon in half and scoop out the seeds. Using a melon baller, or spoon, scoop the flesh out of the shell. Reserve two large pieces of melon for decoration. Purée the remaining flesh together with the orange juice, grape juice, and ground almonds.

Pour the juice into tall glasses. Make a cut in each piece of melon and perch one on the rim of each glass. Decorate the glasses with the orange peel spirals and serve.

Ingredients for 2 drinks:
1 orange
1/2 cantaloupe melon
100ml (3 1/2 fl oz) white grape juice
1 tbsp ground almonds

EQUIPMENT: LEMON SQUEEZER • HAND-HELD BLENDER • 2 TALL GLASSES

Cantaloupe Melon

Of all the melon family, cantaloupe contains the most carotinoids, which help to keep the body's cells healthy, so you should use this in preference to any other melon. Make sure that the melon is ripe; the base should smell strongly of melon and should give way slightly if you press it with your thumb.

power

Dill-Vegetable

full of potassium to aid detoxification

Drink

Rinse the dill and pat it dry. Reserve a few sprigs for garnish. Strip the dill fronds from the stalks. Chop them finely. Peel the cucumber and slice it thickly, reserving two slices for garnish.

Ingredients for 2 drinks:
1 bunch of fresh dill
1 small cucumber
200ml (7fl oz) tomato juice
100ml (3½ fl oz) carrot juice
Cayenne pepper

Purée the cucumber, dill, tomato juice, and carrot juice until smooth. Season to taste with cayenne pepper. Pour the drink into tall glasses. Make a cut from the middle to the edge of each slice of cucumber, and perch one on the rim of each glass. Alternatively, leave the cucumber slices whole and spear them on a cocktail stick, then balance them across the rim of each glass.

EQUIPMENT: HAND-HELD BLENDER • 2 TALL GLASSES

GARNISHING TIP: Cut a whole cucumber in half lengthwise. Using a vegetable peeler, peel off thin strips of cucumber. Take a cherry tomato and sprig of dill, and wrap the strip of cucumber around them. Spear the package on a cocktail stick, then add another cherry tomato, and lay the cocktail stick across the rim of the glass.

Dill on demand

Fresh dill doesn't keep long and dried dill doesn't have the same flavour. For a ready supply of dill, chop fresh dill finely, then freeze it.

Spicy

a wealth of essential nutrients

Vegetable Drink

Cut the red pepper in half. Remove the seeds and membranes and rinse each pepper half. Chop them small. Rinse the parsley and pat it dry. Strip the leaves from the stalks, reserving a few leaves for garnish. Purée the parsley, chopped red pepper, tomato juice, and meat stock.

Season to taste with Tabasco, lemon juice, salt, and pepper. Pour the drink into tall glasses. Garnish with the parsley leaves, and serve immediately.

Ingredients for 2 drinks:
1 red pepper
1/2 bunch of fresh parsley
200ml (7fl oz) tomato juice
200ml (7fl oz) hot chicken stock
Tabasco sauce
Lemon juice
Salt
Freshly ground pepper

EQUIPMENT: HAND-HELD BLENDER • 2 LARGE GLASSES

VARIATION: Try combining vegetable stock and carrot juice for this drink, instead of the meat stock and tomato juice. Omit the Tabasco sauce and lemon juice, and season instead with a pinch of mild curry powder.

GARNISHING TIP: Cut two thick strips from the pepper halves and add them to the drink as edible swizzle sticks.

Peppers

Red peppers contain more vitamin C than green peppers. They are also extremely rich in beta-carotene. Brown marks on the skin, however, indicate that the pepper is no longer completely fresh.

power

Fruit Fantasy

boosts the digestion and metabolism

Cocktail

Ingredients for 2 drinks: • 100 ml (3½ fl oz) pickled cabbage juice • 100ml (3½ fl oz) pineapple juice • 200 ml (7fl oz) apple juice • 2 pieces of fresh or canned pineapple and 2 pieces of apple • fresh mint leaves

Combine the cabbage juice with the pineapple and apple juices, and mix well. Pour the drink into two tall glasses. Cut a slit in each piece of pineapple and apple, and perch one of each on the rim of each glass. Rinse the mint leaves and pat them dry. Garnish the cocktail with the mint leaves, and serve with a straw.

EQUIPMENT: 2 TALL GLASSES • 2 STRAWS

power

White, Red & Green

Italian style

Drink

Ingredients for 2 drinks: • 1 bunch of fresh basil • 200ml (7fl oz) tomato juice • 150g (5oz) natural whole milk yoghurt • balsamic vinegar • olive oil • freshly ground pepper • salt • cherry tomatoes

Wash the basil and pat dry, then strip the leaves. Reserve a few leaves, then chop the rest finely. Purée them with the tomato juice and yoghurt. Season the purée to taste with balsamic vinegar, olive oil, pepper, and salt, then pour into tall glasses. Wash a couple of cherry tomatoes, then make a slit in each, and perch one on the rim of each glass. Garnish with the reserved basil leaves and serve.

EQUIPMENT: HAND-HELD BLENDER • 2 TALL GLASSES

power

Fresh

with vitamins A, C, and E for the immune system

Spring Breeze

Wash the nectarine and pat it dry. Cut it in half, and remove the stone.
Slice a few thin segments from the nectarine halves, and reserve them for
decoration.

Peel the nectarine halves and purée with the ground
almonds, grapefruit, orange, and pear juices until
very smooth and frothy. Pour the cocktail into tall
glasses. To decorate the cocktails, make a cut in each
of the nectarine segments and perch them on the
rim of the glass. Serve immediately.

EQUIPMENT: HAND-HELD BLENDER • 2 TALL GLASSES

Ingredients for 2 drinks:

1 nectarine
1 tbsp ground almonds
100ml (3¹/2 fl oz) grapefruit juice
100ml (3¹/2 fl oz) orange juice
100ml (3¹/2 fl oz) pear juice

VARIATION: You could also prepare this drink using peach or mango. Peel
the mango, and then cut away the flesh from the stone with a flexible
knife. Purée the flesh together with the juices.

DECORATION TIP: You could decorate the rim of the glass with coconut
flakes or desiccated coconut rather than nectarine slices. First dip the rim
of the glass in pear juice, then in the coconut. Pour the drink into the
glasses carefully.

Radish-
with carotinoids and vitamin C
Kohlrabi Cocktail

Ingredients for 2 drinks: • 6 radishes • 1/2 small kohlrabi • 100ml (3¹/2 fl oz) celery juice • 200ml (7fl oz)

koumiss • celery salt • pepper • 2 celery stalks

Rinse and scrub the radishes. Rinse the kohlrabi and peel it. Chop them both finely, and purée

them with the celery juice. Pass the purée through a sieve, and add it to the koumiss, mixing

well. Season to taste with celery salt and pepper. Pour into glasses. Trim and wash the celery.

Garnish each glass with a stalk of celery, and serve. Substitute yoghurt if koumiss is unavailable.

EQUIPMENT: HAND-HELD BLENDER • SIEVE • 2 TALL GLASSES

power

Rose-Red
three-pronged defence: beta-carotene, vitamin C, and lactic acid
Koumiss Drink

Ingredients for 2 drinks: • 100 ml (3¹/2 fl oz) fermented beetroot juice • 100ml (3¹/2 fl oz) koumiss

• 100ml (3¹/2 fl oz) carrot juice • 100ml (3¹/2 fl oz) blackcurrant juice • freshly ground pepper • salt

• ground coriander

Mix together the beetroot juice, koumiss, carrot, and blackcurrant juice. Season to taste with

pepper, salt, and ground coriander. Pour the koumiss drink into tall glasses and serve with a

straw. Substitute yoghurt if koumiss is unavailable.

EQUIPMENT: 2 TALL GLASSES • 2 STRAWS

Quick & Easy
for pure pleasure
Drink

Peel the mango. Using a flexible knife, cut the flesh away from the stone, then chop the flesh into small pieces. Purée the mango together with the grapefruit, pineapple, and grape juices. Heat a frying pan, and dry-fry the desiccated or grated coconut in it until golden brown. To decorate, first dip the rim of each glass in pineapple juice, then in toasted coconut. Carefully pour the drink into the glasses. Sprinkle the remaining toasted coconut and the vanilla sugar on top. Serve with a straw.

Ingredients for 2 drinks:

1 small mango
100ml (3½ fl oz) grapefruit juice
100ml (3½ fl oz) pineapple juice
100ml (3½ fl oz) grape juice
Desiccated or grated coconut
Vanilla sugar

EQUIPMENT: HAND-HELD BLENDER • 2 LARGE GLASSES • 2 STRAWS

DECORATING TIP: Toss a slice of mango in the toasted coconut and leave to dry. Then perch the slice of mango on the rim of the glass.

Mango

This exotic fruit contains lots of protective vitamins and thus strengthens the body's defences. In the middle is a large, hard stone. To separate the flesh from the stone, cleanly peel the mango. Then, using a sharp, flexible boning knife, cut slices from the flesh, working around the mango. Incidentally, the colour of a mango's skin is not always a guide to its ripeness.

Mango Yoghurt Ice
in Pineapple Koumiss

low fat energy booster for hot days

In a saucepan, bring the sugar and water to the boil. Leave to cool, then refrigerate. Wash and dry the lime. Using a sharp knife or canelle knife, remove the peel in a very thin spiral. Cut the lime in half and squeeze out the juice. Peel the mango. Cut the flesh away from the stone with a flexible knife, and cut the flesh into pieces. Purée the fruit, cold sugar syrup, lime juice, and yoghurt.

Ingredients for 2 drinks:
2 tbsp sugar
2 tbsp water
1 lime
1/2 mango
100ml (3½ fl oz) low fat live yoghurt
200ml (7fl oz) pineapple juice
200ml (7fl oz) koumiss

Immediately pour the mixture into a shallow freezer-proof container, and freeze for about 4 hours, stirring thoroughly from time to time to break up the ice crystals. Mix together the pineapple juice and koumiss and pour it into tall glasses. Scoop out balls of mango yoghurt ice and float them in the pineapple koumiss. Decorate with the lime peel spirals and serve. Substitute additional yoghurt if koumiss is unavailable.

EQUIPMENT: HAND-HELD BLENDER • 3-STAR FREEZER OR ICE BOX • 2 TALL GLASSES

VARIATION: Instead of mango, wash 200g (7oz) strawberries, raspberries or blueberries, and pat them dry. Pick them over, then purée them with the yoghurt. Flavour the ice with 2 tbsp desiccated or grated coconut and 1 tbsp grated chocolate, instead of the lime.

power

Caribbean Coconut
with the sharpness of grapefruit
Cocktail

Wash the nectarine and pat it dry. Cut it in half, and remove the stone. Peel the papaya, then cut it in half, and scoop out the seeds. Wash the grapefruit and cut it in half. Cut two segments

Ingredients for 2 drinks:
- 1 nectarine
- 1 small papaya
- 1 grapefruit
- 2 tbsp desiccated or grated coconut or
- 2 tsp coconut syrup
- 100ml (3 1/2 fl oz) grape juice, chilled
- Mineral water, chilled
- Grated coconut

from one half of the grapefruit, and reserve them for decoration. Squeeze the juice from the grapefruit.

Purée the flesh from the nectarine and papaya together with the coconut or coconut syrup, grape juice, and grapefruit juice. Pour the drink into tall glasses, and dilute with mineral water to taste, if necessary. Sprinkle grated or desiccated coconut over the cocktail. Make a slit in each of the grapefruit segments, and perch one on the rim of each glass. Serve immediately.

EQUIPMENT: LEMON SQUEEZER • HAND-HELD BLENDER • 2 TALL GLASSES

VARIATION: You can prepare the cocktail with mango instead of papaya. Peel the mango and cut the flesh away from the stone. Purée the flesh with the other ingredients, as described above.

Papaya

This tropical fruit provides the defensive vitamins A and C, which provide protection from colds and the harmful effects of the sun's rays. Papaya skin should be yellowish-orange, indicating ripeness.

power

Good Mood
for first thing in the morning and last thing at night
Mixture

Ingredients for 2 drinks: • 100ml (3 1/2 fl oz) white grape juice • 3 oranges • 100ml (3 1/2 fl oz) pear juice

Pour enough grape juice to make 4-6 cubes into an ice cube tray, and freeze for about 4 hours.

Cut the oranges in half, then cut off 2 slices and reserve them. Squeeze the oranges. Mix the

orange juice with the remaining grape juice and pear juice. Place 2-3 grape juice cubes in each

glass. Pour the juice mixture over the ice. Make a cut in each slice of orange from the middle to

the edge. Perch a slice of orange on the rim of each glass and serve.

EQUIPMENT: LEMON SQUEEZER • ICE CUBE TRAY • 3-STAR FREEZER OR ICE BOX• 2 TALL GLASSES

Pink Kiwi
over crushed ice
Colada

Ingredients for 2 drinks: • 1 papaya • 4 kiwi fruit • 100ml (3 1/2 fl oz) cherry juice • 100ml (3 1/2 fl oz) pear

juice • soda water • 4 ice cubes

Peel the papaya, then cut it in half and scoop out the seeds. Peel the kiwi fruit. Purée the papaya

and kiwi fruit until very smooth, then mix the purée with the cherry and pear juices. Dilute the

mixture to taste with soda water. Put the ice cubes in a freezer bag and smash them with a

rolling pin. Divide the crushed ice between tall glasses. Pour the cocktail over the crushed ice.

Serve with straws.

EQUIPMENT: • HAND-HELD BLENDER • FREEZER BAG • 2 TALL GLASSES • 2 STRAWS

Strawberry-Mango

refreshing and energizing

Cooler

Wash the strawberries, hull them, and leave them to drain on a tea-towel. Peel the mango. Cut the flesh away from the stone with a flexible knife, then chop the flesh into small pieces. Wash

Ingredients for 2 drinks:
100g (3½ oz) strawberries
1 small mango
2 limes
100ml (3½ fl oz) chilled grape juice
100ml (3½ fl oz) chilled apple juice
Chilled mineral water

and dry the limes. Remove the peel from the limes in a very thin spiral. Cut the limes in half and squeeze out the juice. Slice a few of the strawberries and reserve them for decoration. Purée the remaining strawberries and mango with the lime, grape, and apple juices. Add a little mineral water if liked. Pour the strawberry-mango cooler into tall glasses. Decorate with the lime peel spirals and sliced strawberries and serve.

EQUIPMENT: LEMON SQUEEZER • HAND-HELD BLENDER • 2 TALL GLASSES

 ### Preparing mango

You don't have to peel the mango. Instead, first slice through all the flesh on either side of the stone. Carefully score each mango half, on the flesh side, in a chequerboard pattern, taking care not to cut through the skin. Hold the piece of mango by the edges in both hands, skin side uppermost, and press down gently but firmly on the skin with the thumbs. It should turn inside out. The flesh should still be attached to the skin, and should stand proud of the skin in chunks. Now you can cut the flesh away from the skin.

power

Sun-Blocker

lots of beta-carotene to protect the skin

Cocktail

Ingredients for 2 drinks: • 1 mango • 100ml (3½ fl oz) pineapple juice • 100ml (3½ fl oz) carrot juice • 100ml (3½ fl oz) apple juice • ice cubes

Peel the mango. Cut off a slice and reserve it for decoration, then separate the remaining flesh from the stone, chop it small, and purée it. Add the pineapple, carrot, and apple juices. Put the ice cubes in tall glasses and pour the cocktail over them. Divide the slice of mango into two large pieces, and perch one on the rim of each glass.

EQUIPMENT: HAND-HELD BLENDER • 2 TALL GLASSES

power
Highway
with lots of essential nutrients
to Holiday

Ingredients for 2 drinks: • 1 banana • 1 mango • 150ml (5fl oz) pineapple juice • tonic water

Peel the banana and mango. Separate the mango flesh from the stone. Finely chop the mango and banana, and purée them with the pineapple juice. If the mixture is too thick, add a splash of tonic water. Pour into tall glasses, add a straw, and serve.

EQUIPMENT: HAND-HELD BLENDER • 2 LARGE GLASSES • 2 WIDE STRAWS

Slight

with cantaloupe melon purée

Summer Dream

Pour enough grape juice into an ice cube tray to make 4-6 ice cubes, and freeze it. Cut the melon in half and scoop out the seeds with a spoon. Carefully remove the flesh from the rind and chop the flesh into small pieces.

Peel the mango and remove the flesh from the stone with a sharp knife. Chop the flesh into small pieces. Purée the mango, melon, pineapple juice, and remaining grape juice. Put 2 or 3 cubes of frozen grape juice in each glass. Pour the fruit cocktail over the ice. Wash the grapes, pat them dry, and hang them over the rim of each glass. Serve with a straw.

Ingredients for 2 drinks:
100ml (3½ fl oz) white grape juice
1/2 cantaloupe melon
1 mango
200ml (7fl oz) pineapple juice
2 small clusters white grapes

EQUIPMENT: HAND-HELD BLENDER • 2 LARGE GLASSES • 2 STRAWS

DECORATING TIP: Put a small, seedless grape in each ice cube section with the grape juice. The ice cubes will look prettier.

Grapes

Grapes, especially dark red or black grapes, contain large quantities of healthy plant dyes, which keep the heart and circulation young and in good shape. The more of these so-called flavonoids you eat or drink, the lower the risk of suffering a heart attack. They may even help to prevent cancers.

power

Green Card
endless essential nutrients
Cocktail

Wash the dill and chives and pat them dry. Strip the dill fronds from the stalks, and
chop them finely. Chop the chives into short lengths. Reserve about 1 tsp of chopped
herbs for decoration.

Cut the avocado in half lengthwise and take out the stone. Cut
off two slices of avocado and reserve them for garnish. Scrape
the avocado flesh out of the shell, and purée it with the
chopped herbs and koumiss.

If the puree is too thick, add a splash of mineral water. Season
the cocktail to taste with lemon juice, cardamom, salt, and
pepper.

Pour the cocktail into tall glasses. Make an incision in each slice
of avocado so it can be perched on the rim of a glass. Sprinkle the reserved chopped
herbs over the cocktail, and serve immediately.

EQUIPMENT: HAND-HELD BLENDER • 2 TALL GLASSES

Ingredients for 2 drinks:
1 bunch of fresh dill
1 bunch of fresh chives
1 avocado
400ml (14fl oz) koumiss
Mineral water
Lemon juice
Ground cardamom
Salt
Freshly ground white pepper

Snipping herbs

You can chop dill and chives more quickly using
kitchen scissors. Grasp a bunch of chives in your
hand, and cut off short lengths with the scissors. It is
easy to separate dill fronds from the stalk with sharp,
pointed scissors.

Berry Bowl
with seasonal berries
with Fruit Juice

Wash the berries, remove any stalks, sort them, and leave them to drain on a tea-towel. Cut any large berries in half. Wash the lime and pat it dry. Using a sharp knife or canelle knife, remove

Ingredients for 2 drinks:
2 tbsp berries of your choice
1 lime
100ml (3½ fl oz) cherry juice
100ml (3½ fl oz) blackcurrant juice
200ml (7fl oz) tonic water

the peel in a long, thin spiral. Cut the lime in half and squeeze out the juice. Mix the lime juice, cherry juice, and blackcurrant juice together well, and top up with tonic water. Pour the drink into tall glasses. Add the berries and decorate with some of the lime spiral. Serve immediately.

EQUIPMENT: LEMON SQUEEZER • 2 TALL GLASSES

DECORATING TIP: Dredge large berries in icing sugar and grated coconut, then perch them on the rims of the glasses. Fruit punches can be served with a little cocktail stick on which a cocktail cherry, slice of lime, and a berry have been speared.

Raspberries
In addition to their wonderful flavour raspberries contain lots vitamins, minerals, roughage, and other essential nutrients. These help to boost your defences, promote the digestion, and strengthen the heart and circulation.

Red Pepper

push-ups for body and mind

Power

Ingredients for 2 drinks: • 1 red pepper • 100ml (3½ fl oz) carrot juice • 100ml (3½ fl oz) pineapple juice • 100ml (3½ fl oz) grape juice • mild curry powder

Wash the pepper, cut it in half, and remove the stalk, seeds, and membranes. Either purée the pepper with the juices and pass the mixture through a sieve, or squeeze the juice from the pepper and blend it with the other juices. Pour into tall glasses, and sprinkle a little curry powder on top.

Equipment: Hand-held Blender or Juicer • 2 Tall Glasses

Broccoli, Pear &

with pickled cabbage juice

Pineapple Juice

Ingredients for 2 drinks: • 200g (7oz) broccoli florets • 100ml (3½ fl oz) pineapple juice • 100ml (3½ fl oz) pear juice • 100ml (3½ fl oz) pickled cabbage juice • ground ginger

Wash the broccoli florets and reserve two for garnish. Either purée the remaining florets with the juices, and push the purée through a sieve, or extract the juice from the broccoli and mix it with the pineapple, pear, and cabbage juices. Make an incision in the stalk of each broccoli floret, and perch one on the rim of each tall glass. Pour the juice into the glasses and garnish with a sprinkling of ground ginger. Serve immediately.

Equipment: Hand-held Blender or Juicer • 2 Tall Glasses

Vitality

with aromatic three-fruit purée

Fruit Cocktail

Peel the banana. Wash the blueberries and pick them over. Cut the nectarine in half, remove the stone, and peel the flesh. Cut off a few slices of banana for decoration and reserve them with a few blueberries, and small slices of nectarine.

Purée the fruit with the pear juice and koumiss. If the drink is too thick, dilute it with a little mineral water. Season to taste with cinnamon. Pour the drink into tall glasses and sprinkle a little ground cinnamon and cocoa powder on top.

Alternately spear slices of banana, blueberries, and slices of nectarine on a cocktail stick. Lay the cocktail stick across the rim of the glass, and serve. Substitute with yoghurt if koumiss is unavailable.

Ingredients for 2 drinks:
1 banana
100g (3½ oz) blueberries
1 nectarine
100ml (3½ fl oz) pear juice
100ml (3½ fl oz) koumiss
Mineral water
Ground cinnamon
Cocoa powder

EQUIPMENT: HAND-HELD BLENDER • 2 COCKTAIL STICKS • 2 LARGE GLASSES

DECORATING TIP: Dip the rim of the glass in pear juice, and then dip it immediately in cocoa powder or ground cinnamon. Carefully pour the fruit cocktail into the glasses, and serve.

power

Night Owl
with enlivening parsley
Cocktail

Ingredients for 2 drinks: • 200ml (7fl oz) apple juice • Tabasco sauce • lemon juice • freshly ground pepper • 6 sprigs of parsley

Blend together the tomato and apple juices, then season to taste with a drop of Tabasco, a few drops of lemon juice, and freshly ground pepper. Wash the parsley and pat it dry. Chop half of it very finely and mix it into the drink. Pour the drink into the glasses and garnish with the remaining parsley.

EQUIPMENT: 2 LARGE COCKTAIL GLASSES

power
Drive-in
magnesium to strengthen the muscles
Drink

Ingredients for 2 drinks: • 1 banana • 75ml (3fl oz) tomato juice • 75ml (3fl oz) orange juice • 75ml (3fl oz) grapefruit juice • 75ml (3fl oz) pineapple juice • ground cloves • 2 cherry tomatoes • 2 pieces of pineapple

Peel the banana, chop it into small pieces and purée it with the tomato, orange, grapefruit, and pineapple juices. Season to taste with a pinch of ground cloves, and pour into tall glasses. Make an incision in each of the cherry tomatoes and pieces of pineapple, and perch one of each on the rim of each glass. Serve with straws.

EQUIPMENT: HAND-HELD BLENDER • 2 TALL GLASSES • 2 STRAWS

power

Apricot & Apple Whey

keeps the metabolism in good order

Drink

Wash the apricots, cut them in half, and remove the stones. Reserve 2 apricot halves for decoration. Chop the remaining apricots into small pieces. Purée the apricots and apple juice with the whey, then press the mixture through a fine sieve, if necessary. Flavour the whey drink with vanilla sugar, to taste, and pour into large glasses. Cut each reserved apricot half in half again. Make an incision in each quarter, perch two quarters on the rim of each glass, and serve. Substitute buttermilk if whey is unavailable.

EQUIPMENT: HAND-HELD BLENDER • SIEVE • 2 LARGE GLASSES

Ingredients for 2 drinks:

6 apricots
200ml (7fl oz) apple juice
150ml (5fl oz) whey
Vanilla sugar
to taste

DECORATING TIP: Wash a small appple, remove the core with an apple corer, and cut the apple into thin rounds. Dip the slices of apple in lemon juice to prevent them from discolouring. Make an incision in each slice of apple, and perch a couple on the edge of a glass with the slices of apricot.

Whey

Whey is the liquid which is left over after making cheese. We are more familiar with it as the clear liquid that floats at the top of yoghurt. It contains lactic acid, as well as valuable proteins, which can help promote better digestion.

Kiwi Fruit Shake

with vitamin C and beta-carotene

with Melon Ice

In a saucepan, bring the sugar and water to a boil, remove from the heat and allow the syrup to cool, then chill it in the refrigerator. Peel 2 kiwi fruit and chop them into pieces. Cut the melon in half, remove the seeds, then scoop out the flesh with a spoon or melon baller. Purée the fruit with the chilled sugar syrup and yoghurt. Transfer the mixture immediately to a shallow, freezer-proof container, and freeze for at least 4 hours, stirring occasionally to break up the ice crystals.

Peel the remaining kiwi fruit and purée them with the hand-held blender. Dilute the purée with mineral water. Slit the vanilla pod in half lengthwise, scrape out the seeds with a pointed knife, and add them to the kiwi fruit and mineral water mixture. Place 1 scoop of melon ice in a large glass, top up with the kiwi fruit drink, and serve immediately.

EQUIPMENT: HAND-HELD BLENDER • 3-STAR FREEZER OR ICE BOX • 2 LARGE GLASSES

Ingredients for 2 drinks:
2 tbsp sugar
2 tbsp water
5 kiwi fruit
1/2 small cantaloupe melon
150ml (5fl oz) low fat bio yoghurt
200ml (7fl oz) mineral water
1 vanilla pod

Fruit enzymes

Fresh kiwi fruit, mangoes, and pineapple contain enzymes which split proteins. This is why dishes which combine these fruits and gelatine won't set, or why fromage frais or yoghurt combined with these fruits tastes sour. To prevent the enzymes in this shake getting to work, the fruit and yoghurt purée must be frozen immediately.

Berry-

with lecithin and minerals for the nerves

Banana Shake

Peel the banana and cut off a few slices. Reserve them for decoration. Cut the remaining

banana into small pieces. Wash the berries thoroughly, pick them over, and leave them to drain

Ingredients for 2 drinks:

1 banana

150g (5oz) blackberries
(or other berries)

2 tbsp ground almonds

300ml (10fl oz) buttermilk

Mineral water

Ground cinnamon

on a tea-towel, reserving a few.

Purée the remaining berries with the chopped banana, ground

almonds, and buttermilk. If the drink is too thick, dilute to taste

with mineral water.

Season the drink with a pinch of ground cinnamon. Pour into

large glasses. Decorate with the reserved banana slices and

berries, and serve.

EQUIPMENT: HAND-HELD BLENDER • 2 LARGE GLASSES

VARIATION: You can turn this shake into a long cool summer drink by adding some crushed ice

to each glass.

Banana

Of all the varieties of fruit, bananas are as

popular as apples. Bananas lend sweetness

and a creamy, smooth taste, which children

find particularly enjoyable, to every drink.

Bananas contain magnesium and vitamin B_6,

which are important for healthy nerves and

muscles.

power

Sweet
for an energy-packed snack
Buttermilk Shake

Ingredients for 2 drinks: • 200ml (7fl oz) buttermilk • 100ml (3½ fl oz) pineapple juice • 100ml (3½ fl oz) grape juice • 2 vanilla pods • 2 long cinnamon sticks

Mix together the buttermilk, pineapple juice, and grape juice. Slit the vanilla pods in half lengthwise, and scrape out the seeds with a knife point. Add them to the buttermilk shake and stir well. Serve in large glasses with the cinnamon sticks and straws.

EQUIPMENT: • 2 LARGE GLASSES • 2 WIDE STRAWS

Fruity
with refreshing koumiss
Strawberry Shake

Ingredients for 2 drinks: • 200g (7oz) strawberries • 2 tbsp koumiss • 100ml (3½ fl oz) grape juice • 100ml (3½ fl oz) orange juice • 1 vanilla pod

Wash the strawberries, hull them, and leave them to drain. Purée the strawberries, koumiss, grape juice, and orange juice, using a hand-held blender. Cut the vanilla pod in half lengthwise, and scrape out the seeds. Add them to the shake and mix well. Pour into large glasses and serve. Substitute with yoghurt if koumiss is unavailable.

EQUIPMENT: HAND-HELD BLENDER • 2 LARGE GLASSES

Rasberry-
with lots of calcium for strong bones
Buttermilk Shake

Pour the grape juice into an ice cube tray, put it in the freezer, and leave it to set.
Wash the raspberries thoroughly, pick them over, and leave them to drain on a tea-

Ingredients for 2 drinks:
50ml (2fl oz) grape juice
150g (5oz) raspberries
50ml (2fl oz) pear juice
200ml (7fl oz) buttermilk
Chilled mineral water
A few seedless white grapes

towel. Reserve a few for decoration. Purée the
raspberries with the pear juice and the buttermilk. If
the mixture is too thick, dilute it to taste with chilled
mineral water. Turn out the grape juice cubes into 2
large glasses, and pour over the buttermilk shake.
Wash the grapes, leave them to drain, take them off
the stalks, and cut them in half. Garnish the shakes

with the halved grapes, and raspberries. Serve immediately.

**EQUIPMENT: HAND-HELD BLENDER • ICE CUBE TRAY • 3-STAR FREEZER OR ICE BOX • 2 LARGE
GLASSES**

VARIATION: To make a cool summer drink you can also use frozen raspberries. Let the
raspberries defrost and purée with the pear and grape juices, then mix in the
buttermilk.

Cold ice cubes cool slower

If the ice cubes are starting to thaw a little, then their
coldness will transfer to the shake faster. The bigger,
and colder, the ice-cubes, the longer they take to
melt, and the more slowly they cool down a drink.

Buttermilk
with cherry and pineapple juices
Coconut Shake

Ingredients for 2 drinks: • 1 vanilla pod • 1 tbsp coconut syrup or 2 tbsp grated coconut • 100ml (3½ fl oz) buttermilk • 200ml (7fl oz) cherry juice • 100ml (3½ fl oz) pineapple juice • grated coconut

Slit the vanilla pod in half lengthwise and scrape out the seeds with a pointed knife. Add the vanilla seeds to the buttermilk with the coconut syrup or grated coconut. Blend together the buttermilk, cherry, and pineapple juices. Dip the rims of 2 large glasses in pineapple juice, then in grated coconut. Carefully pour the drinks into the glasses and serve.

EQUIPMENT: HAND-HELD BLENDER • 2 LARGE GLASSES

power

Yoghurt
cheers you up and gives you energy
Pick-me-up

Ingredients for 2 drinks: • 1 banana • 150ml (5fl oz) yoghurt • 100ml (3½ fl oz) orange juice • vanilla sugar • 50ml (2fl oz) sweetened sea buckthorn juice • cocoa powder • grated chocolate

Peel the banana and purée it with the yoghurt and orange juice. Sweeten to taste with the vanilla sugar. Pour the yoghurt drink into 2 large glasses. Carefully pour over the sea buckthorn juice. Do not stir. Dust thickly with cocoa powder and sprinkle grated chocolate on top. Serve immediately. Substitute the sea buckthorn juice, if unavailable, with 2-3 tsp honey.

EQUIPMENT: HAND-HELD BLENDER • 2 LARGE GLASSES

power

Plum

with natural roughage

Yoghurt Shake

Wash the plums and drain them in a sieve or colander. Cut them in half and remove the stones. Purée the plums with the yoghurt, sugar, and apple juice. If the drink is too thick, dilute it to taste with a little mineral water. Flavour the shake to taste with cinnamon and lemon juice. Pour into large glasses and dust with ground cinnamon. Decorate each glass with 1 cinnamon stick, and serve immediately.

EQUIPMENT: HAND-HELD BLENDER • 2 LARGE GLASSES

Ingredients for 2 drinks:
150g (5oz) plums
200g (7oz) yoghurt
2 tbsp sugar
100ml (3½ fl oz) apple juice
Mineral water
Ground cinnamon
Lemon juice
2 large cinnamon sticks

VARIATION: If you prepare the shake with koumiss, then it will taste more acidic and especially refreshing. You can also make a very creamy version using a large banana instead of the plums.

Yoghurt

You should always use a mild, natural yoghurt for yoghurt-based drinks, but most importantly, it should not have been heat-treated, because this kills the lactic acid bacteria that work in conjunction with the intestinal flora. They prevent diarrhoea and other unpleasant digestive problems. Bio yoghurts are particularly good for regulating your bowels.

power

Banana
with cinnamon and vanilla seeds
Fig Milk

Peel the banana, cut off a couple of slices, and reserve them for decoration. Chop the remaining banana into small pieces. Cut open the figs, scoop out the flesh with a teaspoon, and purée it with the chopped banana and buttermilk until smooth. Cut the vanilla pod in half lengthwise, scrape out the vanilla seeds with a pointed knife, and add them to the buttermilk.

Top up the drink with mineral water, and flavour it to taste with ground cinnamon. Pour the drink into large glasses. Decorate with the reserved banana, dust with a pinch of ground cinnamon, and serve immediately.

Ingredients for 2 drinks:
1 banana
2 fresh figs
200ml (7fl oz) buttermilk
1 vanilla pod
200ml (7fl oz) mineral water
Ground cinnamon

EQUIPMENT: HAND-HELD BLENDER • 2 LARGE GLASSES

GARNISHING TIP: Crush a few ice cubes in a plastic bag, and put the crushed ice in the glasses, then pour over the banana fig milk. Decorate the glasses with slices of fig and banana, and serve with long vanilla pods, and cinnamon sticks.

Know your figs
Unripe figs have no flavour. Look for figs which have a reddish brown, slightly purplish tinge to the skin. Green figs are not ripe enough.

power

Pineapple

B vitamins for energy and strong nerves

Almond Milk

Purée the ground almonds with 50g (2oz) of grated or desiccated coconut, the pineapple juice, milk, and yoghurt. Sweeten to taste with vanilla sugar.

Ingredients for 2 drinks:
3 tbsp ground almonds
70g (2 1/2 oz) grated or desiccated coconut
200ml (7fl oz) pineapple juice
100ml (3 1/2 fl oz) milk
100ml (3 1/2 fl oz) yoghurt
Vanilla sugar

Put the remaining coconut in a non-stick frying pan and dry-fry it until toasted and golden brown. Pour the almond milk into large glasses, then sprinkle the toasted coconut on top. Serve the pineapple almond milk immediately.

EQUIPMENT: HAND-HELD BLENDER • FRYING PAN • 2 LARGE GLASSES

VARIATION: If you like your drinks less sweet, then use grapefruit juice instead of the milk and omit the vanilla sugar.

DECORATING TIP: Take a ring of canned pineapple, drain it and cut it into six segments. Toss the pineapple segments in grated coconut. Perch the pieces of pineapple on the rim of the glass.

Coconut

Grated coconut tastes very good combined with fruit juices, and it is also a great health food due to its high magnesium and iron content. These minerals are required for healthy nerves and muscles.

power

Lamb's Lettuce

carotinoids detoxify the body

Buttermilk Shake

Ingredients for 2 drinks: • 50g (2oz) lamb's lettuce • 3 tbsp ground almonds • 100ml (3½ fl oz) apple juice • 50ml (2fl oz) tomato juice • 200ml (7fl oz) buttermilk • 1 lemon • freshly grated nutmeg

Wash the lamb's lettuce thoroughly, reserving a few small leaves for garnish. Purée the remaining leaves with the ground almonds, apple and tomato juices, and buttermilk. Wash the lemon. Grate the peel very finely. Cut the lemon in half and squeeze out the juice. Flavour the shake to taste with lemon peel, lemon juice, and freshly grated nutmeg.

EQUIPMENT: HAND-HELD BLENDER • LEMON SQUEEZER

Cucumber-Melon

health mix with vitamins and minerals

Milk

Ingredients for 2 drinks: • 1 bunch of fresh dill • 1 cucumber • 1/2 cantaloupe melon • 100ml (3½ fl oz) buttermilk • salt • freshly ground pepper

Wash the dill, shake it dry, and strip the fronds from the stalks. Reserve a few fronds for garnish. Peel and slice the cucumber, reserving a few thick slices. Cut the melon in half, scoop out the seeds, then scoop out the flesh. Purée the cucumber, melon, dill, and buttermilk. Season to taste with salt and pepper, pour into tall glasses, and serve garnished with the cucumber slices and dill fronds.

EQUIPMENT: HAND-HELD BLENDER • 2 TALL GLASSES

Anti-Influenza Punch

with lots of vitamin C

Make the tea with the boiling water and leave it to infuse for 5 minutes. Wash the oranges, dry them, and remove the peel in a very thin spiral, using a sharp knife. Cut the oranges in half and squeeze out the juice.

Strain the tea into a saucepan, add the orange and grapefruit juices, and stir well. Add the star anise and sweeten to taste with sugar.

Heat the mixture through quickly, but do not let it boil. Rinse out two punch glasses, or other heat-resistant glasses, with hot water. Serve the punch in the glasses, decorated with coffee sugar and orange peel spirals.

Ingredients for 2 drinks:
200ml (7fl oz) boiling water
2 tsp Assam tea or 2 tea sachets
2 oranges
100ml (3½ fl oz) grapefruit juice
1 tsp star anise
Sugar
2 tbsp brown sugar

EQUIPMENT: LEMON SQUEEZER • STRAINER • 2 HEAT-RESISTANT PUNCH GLASSES

VARIATION: If you like your punch sweeter, use grape juice instead of grapefruit juice, adding a teaspoon of lemon juice and honey to taste.

Vitamin C

Citrus fruits are rich in vitamin C, so their juice, preferably freshly squeezed so it contains the maximum vitamin C, is used in many health drinks. Blood oranges also contain carotinoids. Both essential nutrients also play a dual role by also effectively protecting the body's cells from aggressive pollutants.

Sweet
tastes good hot or cold
Iron-Man

Ingredients for 2 drinks: • 200ml (7fl oz) cherry juice • 100ml (31/2 fl oz) blackcurrant juice • 100ml (31/2 fl oz) fermented beetroot juice • ground cloves • ground cardamom • 2 sprigs blackcurrants

Mix all the juices together in a saucepan, and heat them through. Add ground cloves and cardamom to taste. Pour the punch into pre-heated glasses. Perch a blackcurrant sprig on the rim of each glass and serve. Use ordinary beetroot juice if the fermented juice is unavailable.

EQUIPMENT: 2 HEAT-RESISTANT GLASSES

power

Winter Delight
just the thing for influenza
Punch

Ingredients for 2 drinks: • 100ml (31/2 fl oz) boiling water • 1 tsp rosehip tea or 1 tea sachet • 100ml (31/2 fl oz) blackcurrant juice • 100ml (31/2 fl oz) grape juice • ground cloves

Pour the boiling water over the rosehip tea or tea sachet and leave it to infuse for 10 minutes. Strain the tea, and combine the infusion with the blackcurrant juice and grape juice. Add a pinch of ground cloves to taste, and serve in warmed punch glasses.

EQUIPMENT: STRAINER • 2 HEAT-RESISTANT PUNCH GLASSES

power

Blue Hour
warm juices for cold snaps
Orchard Cocktail

Rinse the blackberries carefully, pick them over, and leave them on a tea-towel to drain. If you are using frozen blackberries, allow them to defrost. Quickly heat through the grape, blackcurrant, and cherry juices in a saucepan, but do not let them boil. Add the blackberries to the pan, and purée the mixture briefly. Add a pinch of ground cinnamon to taste.

Rinse out 2 heat-resistant glasses with hot water. Pour the punch into them, and serve with long cinnamon sticks.

EQUIPMENT: HAND-HELD BLENDER • 2 HEAT-RESISTANT PUNCH GLASSES

Ingredients for 2 drinks:
150g (5oz) fresh or frozen blackberries
100ml (3 1/2 fl oz) red grape juice
100ml (3 1/2 fl oz) blackcurrant juice
100ml (3 1/2 fl oz) morello cherry juice
Ground cinnamon
2 long cinnamon sticks

VARIATION: You can serve this drink cold, omitting the ground cinnamon and cinnamon stick. Add some sugar or pineapple juice to taste instead.

DECORATING TIP: Alternately spear small pieces of pineapple and blackberries on cocktail sticks, and serve them with the drinks.

Blackberries

Blackberries are best fresh, but are not always available. However, frozen berries still have a very good flavour and contain many minerals such as calcium, magnesium, and iron. They help to strengthen bones and the body's defences.

Camomile-Citrus

helps keep you on your feet

Punch

Ingredients for 2 drinks:
200ml (7fl oz) boiling water
2 tsp camomile tea or 2 tea sachets
1/2 lemon
2 oranges
1 grapefruit
4 tsp sugar

Pour the boiling water over the camomile tea or tea sachets and leave to infuse for 10 minutes. In the meantime, wash the oranges and lemon thoroughly under hot, running water, dry them, and cut off the peel in a very thin spiral, with a sharp knife. Reserve the peel spirals. Cut the grapefruit and the oranges in half, and squeeze out the juice. Strain the camomile tea into a jug and add the lemon, orange, and grapefruit juices. Sweeten to taste with sugar. Rinse out 2 heat-resistant glasses with hot water and pour the punch into them. Decorate the punch with orange and lemon peel spirals, and serve immediately.

EQUIPMENT: LEMON SQUEEZER • 2 HEAT-RESISTANT GLASSES

More squeeze, more juice

To make citrus fruit release as much of their juice as possible, lemons, oranges and grapefruit can be rolled around on a flat surface, with the palm of your hand. The more you squeeze them, the more juice will be released from the flesh.

Fennel-Exotic

to smooth your prickly throat

Fruit Punch

Pour the boiling water over the fennel tea or tea sachets and leave to infuse for 10 minutes. Cut the papaya in half, scoop out the seeds, then peel it, and chop the flesh into small pieces. Cut the piece of melon in half, and cut off two small slices. Scoop out the remaining flesh with a spoon, and purée it with the papaya and pineapple juice. Strain the fennel tea into the fruit mixture. Add a pinch of ground ginger to taste. Rinse out 2 heat-resistant glasses with hot water. Pour the punch into them, and serve immediately.

Ingredients for 2 drinks:
200ml (7fl oz) boiling water
2 tsp fennel tea or 2 tea sachets
1/2 papaya
1/2 cantaloupe melon
100ml (3 1/2 fl oz) pineapple juice
Ground ginger

EQUIPMENT: HAND-HELD BLENDER • 2 HEAT-RESISTANT PUNCH GLASSES

Herbal teas

Herbal teas can be purchased loose or in sachets from supermarkets and health food stores. Fennel tea helps to combat coughs or headaches. Camomile tea prevents inflammations and stomach aches. Sage is good for sore throats, and linden blossom tea helps infections and colds. If neat herbal teas are not to your taste, try a mixture of tea and fruit juice.

power

Sea Buckthorn

with grapefruit juice and aniseed

Sage Punch

Ingredients for 2 drinks: • 200ml (7fl oz) boiling water • 1 tsp sage • 100ml (3½ fl oz) grapefruit juice • 2 tbsp sweetened sea buckthorn juice • 3 tsp honey • ground aniseed • lemon juice

Pour the water over the sage and leave to infuse for 10 minutes. Strain the infusion, and combine it with the grapefruit juice, sea buckthorn juice, and honey. Add aniseed and lemon juice to taste. Pour the punch into heated glasses, and serve immediately. Substitute the sea buckthorn juice, if unavailable, with 2 tsp honey.

EQUIPMENT: STRAINER • 2 HEAT-RESISTANT PUNCH GLASSES

power

Apple-Linden

with pineapple juice and lemon

Blossom Punch

Ingredients for 2 drinks: • 200ml (7fl oz) boiling water • 2 tsp linden blossom tea or 2 tea sachets • 150ml (5fl oz) apple juice • 50ml (2fl oz) pineapple juice • lemon juice • sugar

Pour the boiling water over the linden blossom tea or tea sachets and leave it to infuse for 10 minutes. Strain the tea and mix it with the apple and pineapple juices. Add lemon juice and sugar to taste. Rinse out 2 heat-resistant glasses with hot water. Pour the punch into them and serve immediately.

EQUIPMENT: STRAINER • 2 HEAT-RESISTANT PUNCH GLASSES

power

Rosehip-Blueberry Punch

with active ingredients for stressful days

Pour the boiling water over the rosehip tea, or tea sachets, and leave to infuse for 10 minutes. Wash the blueberries, pick them over, and leave them to drain on a tea-towel. Reserve a few blueberries for decoration; purée the rest. Strain the rosehip tea and combine it with the blackcurrant juice and blueberry purée. Add sugar and ground cinnamon to taste. Rinse out 2 heat-resistant glasses with hot water. Pour the punch into the glasses, add a cinnamon stick and a few blueberries, and serve immediately.

EQUIPMENT: HAND-HELD BLENDER • STRAINER • 2 HEAT-RESISTANT PUNCH GLASSES

Ingredients for 2 drinks:
200ml (7fl oz) boiling water
2 tsp rosehip tea or 2 tea sachets
100g (3½ oz) blueberries
100ml (3½ fl oz) blackcurrant juice
2 tsp sugar
Ground cinnamon
2 long cinnamon sticks

VARIATION: To tickle your tastebuds even more, spice up the punch with 2 coarsely ground cloves and 4 crushed allspice berries. Serve the hot punch with brown sugar and a pinch of star anise.

The spoon trick
You can prevent a glass shattering due to excessive heat if you put a metal spoon in it first. Simply pour the hot punch over the back of the spoon, into the glass. The metal spoon quickly deflects the heat. You should never pour boiling liquid straight into a glass. Even heat-resistant glasses are unlikely to withstand such treatment.

Index to recipes

Energy Drinks-power packed juices, mixed, shaken or stirred

Anti-Influenza Punch 51
Apple-Linden Blossom Punch 57
Apricot & Apple Whey Drink 37

Banana 40
Banana Fig Milk 47
Yoghurt Pick-me-up 44
Berry-Banana Shake 40

Berry Bowl with Fruit Juice 32

Blackberries
Berry-Banana Shake 40
Blue Hour Orchard Cocktail 53

Blue Hour Orchard Cocktail 53
Broccoli, Pear & Pineapple Juice 33

Buttermilk
Banana Fig Milk 47
Berry Banana Shake 40
Buttermilk-Coconut Shake 44
Cucumber-Melon Milk 49
Lamb's Lettuce Buttermilk Shake 49
Raspberry-Buttermilk Shake 42
Sweet Buttermilk Shake 41
White Wellness Shake 12
Camomile-Citrus Punch 54
Cantaloupe Melon 13
Caribbean Coconut Cocktail 24
Coconut 48
Cucumber-Melon Milk 49

Drink Aid 6
Drinks for sportsmen 6
Drinks for the active 6
Drinks for the bowels 7
Drinks for the immune system 7
Drinks for the stomach 7
Drinks to counteract stress 7
Drinks to reduce fluid 6

Drive-in Drink 36

Exotic Energy Cocktail 11

Fennel-Exotic Fruit Punch 56

Figs 47
Banana Fig Milk 47

Fresh Spring Breeze 19
Fruit Fantasy Cocktail 17
Fruity Strawberry Shake 41

Good Mood Mixture 25
Good Morning Alarm Call 13
Grapes 29
Green Card Cocktail 31

Herbal teas 56
Highway to Holiday 28

Kiwi
Exotic Energy Cocktail 11
Kiwi Fruit Shake with Melon Ice 39
Pink Kiwi Colada 25

Koumiss
Green Card Cocktail 31
Radish-Kohlrabi Cocktail 20
Vitality Fruit Cocktail 35

Lamb's Lettuce Buttermilk Drink 49

Mango 21,26
Highway to Holiday 26
Mango Yoghurt Ice in Pineapple
Koumiss 23
Quick & Easy Drink 21
Slight Summer Dream 29
Strawberry-Mango Cooler 26
Sun-Blocker Cocktail 28

Melon
Cucumber-Melon Milk 49
Fennel-Exotic Fruit Punch 56
Good Morning Alarm Call 13
Kiwi Fruit Shake with Melon Ice 39
Slight Summer Dream 29

Abbreviations:

tsp = teaspoon
tbsp = tablespoon

Night Owl Cocktail	36
Orange Juice	
Fresh Spring Breeze	19
Fruity Strawberry Shake	41
Red Panther's Punch	12
Papaya	**24**
Caribbean Coconut Cocktail	24
Exotic Energy Cocktail	11
Pink Kiwi Colada	25
Red Panther's Punch	12
Peppers	**16**
Red Pepper Power	33
Spicy Vegetable Drink	16
Pineapple Almond Milk	48
Plum Yoghurt Shake	45
Pink Kiwi Colada	25
Quick & Easy Drink	21
Radish-Kohlrabi Cocktail	20
Raspberries	**32**
Berry Bowl with Fruit Juice	32
Raspberry-Buttermilk Shake	42
Red Panther's Punch	12
Red Pepper Power	33
Rosehip-Blueberry Punch	59
Rose-Red Koumiss Drink	20
Sea Buckthorn-Sage Punch	57
Slight Summer Dream	29
Spicy Vegetable Drink	16
Strawberry-Mango Cooler	26
Sun-Blocker Cocktail	28
Sweet Buttermilk Shake	41
Sweet Iron-Man	52
Tomato Juice	
Dill-Vegetable Drink	14

Night Owl Cocktail	36
Spicy Vegetable Drink	16
White, Red & Green Drink	17
Vitamin C	**51**
Vitality Fruit Cocktail	35
Whey	**37**
Apricot & Apple Whey Drink	37
White Red & Green Drink	17
White Wellness Shake	12
Winter Delight Punch	52
Yoghurt	**45**
Mango Yoghurt Ice in Pineapple	
Koumiss	23
Plum Yoghurt Shake	45
Yoghurt Pick-me-up	44

Most of the ingredients required for the recipes in this book are easily available from supermarkets and health food stores. In case of difficulty, contact the following importers of organic German produce:-
The Organic Food Company, Unit 2, Blacknest Industrial Estate, Blacknest Road,
Alton GU34 4PX;
(T) 01420 520530 (F) 01420 23985

Windmill Organics, 66 Meadow Close, London SW20 9JD
(T) 0181 395 9749 (F) 0181 286 4732

Fermented Wheat Juice is produced in Germany by Kanne Brottrunk GMBH
(T) 00 49 2592 97400 (F) 00 49 2592 61370

Further information on German food importers is available from The Central Marketing Organisation
(T) 0181 944 0484 (F) 0181 944 0441

Caution

The techniques and recipes in this book
are to be used at the reader's sole
discretion and risk.
Always consult a doctor if you are in doubt
about a medical condition.

Friedrich Bohlmann

Friedrich works as a nutritionist and
dietician and for years has written
specialist articles for major German
journals. He is the resident nutritional
expert on the daytime TV programme
Leben und Wohnen. He has written several
nutritional guides. He has been awarded
the Deutsche Gesellschaft für Ernährung
Journalist's Award.

Photos: FoodPhotography Eising, Munich

Susie M. and **Pete Eising** have studios in
Munich and Kennebunkport, Maine, USA.
They studied at the Munich Academy of
Photography, where they established their
own studio for food photography in 1991.

Food styling: **Monika Schuster**

Vitamin Diet

Lose weight naturally with fresh fruit and vegetables
Angelika Ilies
£4.99
ISBN 1 85675 145 7
All the benefits of eating fresh fruit and vegetables plus a natural way to weight loss.

Energy Drinks

Power-packed juices, mixed, shaken or stirred
Friedrich Bohlmann
£4.99
ISBN 1 85675 140 6
Fresh juices packed full of goodness for vitality and health

Detox

Foods to cleanse and purify from within
Angelika Ilies
£4.99
ISBN 1 85675 150 3
Detoxify your body as part of your daily routine by eating nutritional foods that have cleansing properties

Anti Stress

Recipes for Acid-Alkaline Balance
Dagmar von Cramm
£4.99
ISBN 1 85675 155 4
A balanced diet to reduce stress levels, maximise immunity and help you keep fit

For a catalogue of titles please call 01453 752985 or visit our website www.gaiabooks.co.uk

GAIA